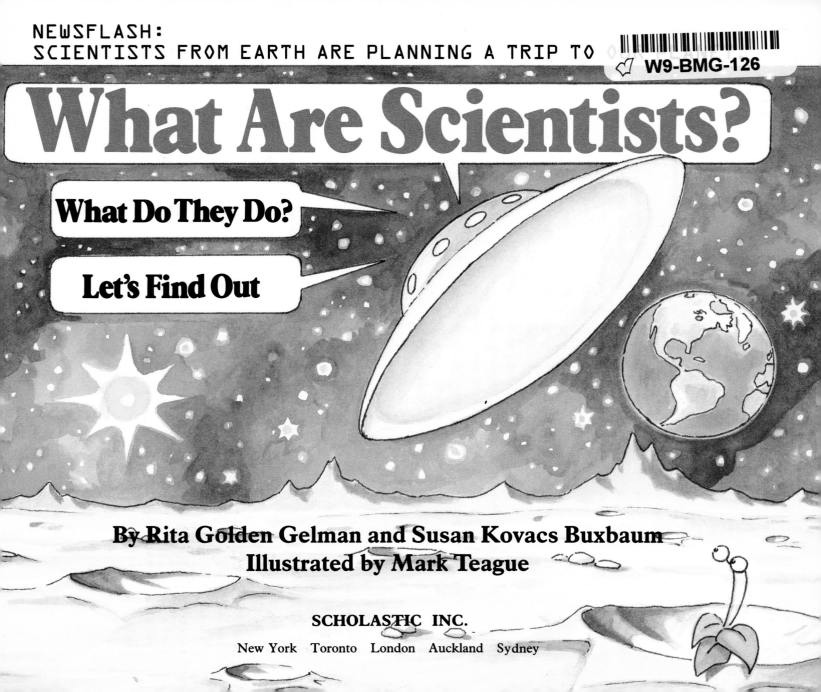

ISBN 0-590-43184-6

Text copyright © 1991 by Rita Golden Gelman and
Susan Kovacs Buxbaum.
Illustrations copyright © 1991 by Mark Teague.
All rights reserved. Published by Scholastic Inc.

12 11 10 9 8 7 6 5 4 3          1 2 3 4 5 6/9

Printed in the U.S.A.          08

First Scholastic printing, February 1991

## Scientists Are People

There are fat scientists
and thin scientists.
Tall ones and short ones.
Scientists with ponytails.
Scientists with beards.

Some scientists jog
while others weed.
They watch TV.
They write and read.

LOOK! HIS TONGUE IS BLUE!

THE WORD SCIENTIST COMES FROM THE LATIN WORD SCIENTIA WHICH MEANS "KNOWLEDGE."

They play with their kids.
Eat blueberry pie.
They dance and cook
and laugh and cry.

They snore and hiccup and hug.
Just like all the other humans.

Scientists study **everything:**
Cats and cuts.
Fire and fog.
Magnets.
Earthquakes.
Flowers and smog.

Light and sound.
Rockets.
Stars.
Blood and bones.
Computers.
Cars.

They work in labs.
In schools.
In space.
In forests and oceans
all over the place!

There are
microbiologists,
endocrinologists,
paleontologists,
bacteriologists,
cryobiologists,
meteorologists,
physicists,
chemists.
And that's just
a start.

There are
pediatricians,
lab technicians,
organic chemists,
and mathematicians,
sedimentologists,
lunar geologists,
nuclear physicists,
plant physiologists.

**BIOLOGIST**

**BIOS** MEANS "LIFE" IN GREEK.

**OLOGIST** MEANS "SOMEONE WHO STUDIES."

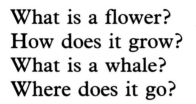

What is a flower?
How does it grow?
What is a whale?
Where does it go?

What is blood?
What does it do?
What makes me me?
What makes you you?

A tree.
A plant.
A rabbit.
A rat.

Biologists study
all of that.

THE LATIN WORD FOR **DOCTOR** MEANS "TEACHER." **DENS** MEANS "TOOTH".

Doctors study coughs
and sneezes.
Cancer and AIDS and
other diseases.
They check your body.
They fix your bumps.
They give you shots.
For measles
and mumps.

DENTIST LIFE

DENTISTS ARE DOCTORS WHO TAKE CARE OF TEETH!

Animals get doctored, too.
That's what veterinarians do.

EARLY CHEMISTS, CALLED ALCHEMISTS, TRIED TO TURN METAL INTO GOLD.

Chemists mix and measure and pour.
They work with $H_2SO_4$.
With $NH_3$ and $HCl$.
With beakers and
test tubes and fire as well.

They know what happens when iron rust
When silver turns to black.
They study changes from gases to liquid
From liquids to solids
and back.

Because of experiments
chemists can do,
we have plastics and
nylon and glasses and glue.
Medicines, ointments, and
aerosol spray.
Millions of things that we
use every day.
(And some that we shouldn't!)

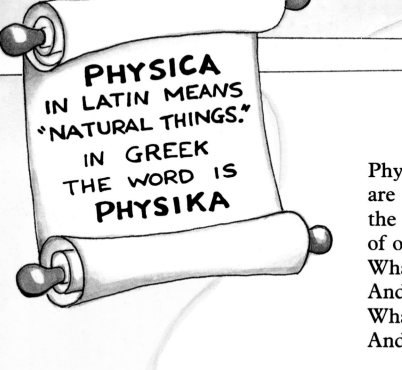

PHYSICA
IN LATIN MEANS
"NATURAL THINGS."
IN GREEK
THE WORD IS
PHYSIKA

Physicists always
are looking to prove
the hows and the whys
of objects that move.
What makes them go?
And why they won't.
What atoms do.
And what they don't.

Computers and rockets
and color TV.
Lasers and stuff
that you can't even see.
Magnets and music
and motors and wings.
Physicists think
about all of those things.

SATURN

JUPITER

MARS

VENUS

MERCURY

SUN

They measure.
They map.
They count.
They view.

Those are the things
that astronomers do.

If the sun were the size of a beach ball,
the earth would be the size of a pea.

Geologists study the stuff of the earth.
And how it came to be.
They study volcanoes and ancient stones.
And mountains under the sea.

Earthquakes, lava, fossils, oil.
Diamonds, silver, rocks, and soil.

When earthquakes shake,
when geysers spout,
when drillers drill
and oil comes out,
when volcanoes explode
or meteors fall,
geologists try
to study them all.

METEORON

IN GREEK MEANS "THING IN THE AIR."

Tornadoes and hurricanes,
lights in the sky.
Meteorologists want to know why.

Drizzle and wind,
blizzards and smog.
Rain and snow and
thunder and fog.

They study typhoons.
They measure monsoons.
With computers and maps
and weather balloons.